ISBN 978-1-4357-9396-5

DALE L. HEATON

REALITY RELIGION

A Biblical Faith Handbook for the Modern World

ACKNOWLEDGEMENTS

This book is dedicated to Jane T. Heaton, my spouse and partner in ministry for fifty-nine years, without whose help, encouragement, and shared thoughts it could not have been written. I also want to thank my son, James D. Heaton, for his proofreading, format, and layout work, as well as arrangement for printing and publication.

In addition, I want to acknowledge and express appreciation to all the people through the years who have deepened my faith through their honest questions, which led to my thinking through this articulation of answers in written form.

I also want to express gratitude to all the readers of the original draft of this treatise who said it was helpful to them and encouraged its publication. I want to thank my brother-in-law, David Threinen, a retired geologist, who said it was terrific and should be published. I thank my twenty-one-year-old college-student grandson, Dunstan Heaton, who said it dealt with questions people have and communicated the subjects in a way that could reach young people helpfully as a way of viewing the faith you can better apply to your life. I want to acknowledge Kari Stiles, a woman who grew up in my ministry, who said she was reading it slowly because it gave her food for thought, and David Gamble, a physician's assistant, who wrote, "You addressed very eloquently answers to so many important subjects I have often questioned and wondered about. You clearly put the Bible in perspective for me." Thank you to Shawn Quinn, a NASA engineer and scientist, who said, "I found it extremely interesting and relevant in today's world and was amazed at how many of the questions you addressed have come up in my own explorations of the faith over the years. Your clear articulation of thoughts is certainly worth publishing for much broader distribution." My thanks to the Rev. Robert Early, who enthusiastically said, "I loved it!" and to Larry Williams, the retired minister from California who said, "This should be shared with younger people." Thanks to Walter Horlander, a retired Florida Council of Churches executive, who said, "It is a writing that should be a study resource in local churches," and to Evons Opoku, a young helicopter pilot in Ghana, who said, "It gave me insight into a lot of things I had no idea about."

My thanks go to a fellow churchman, who early on expressed appreciation for the helpfulness imparted in understandable form to difficult theological questions, particularly in connection with the Trinity. He passed the document on to an out-of-town friend, Rudy Zurl. My special thanks go to Rudy, then a stranger to me, who wrote to say it changed his Biblical world view and had a profound effect upon his life. His affirmations of confidence, his belief in the significance of the work and its effective communication on difficult faith questions, and his insistence on publication enabled this book to become a reality. My appreciation goes also to God as made known through Jesus, the Christ and the faith shared in this book that has sustained me through the years.

DALE L. HEATON

REALITY **RELIGION**

A BIBLICAL FAITH HANDBOOK FOR THE MODERN WORLD

CONTENTS

PREFACE

Many people have questions about the Bible and the faith that they do not feel free to ask, since questioning is often viewed as ignorance or lack of faith. In reality, questions are a sign of intelligence and sincere seeking after faith, a search for answers to doubts. I have always viewed the questions of others as an opportunity to rethink my own faith and reshape my answers to help people over faith obstacles they are encountering. This has become more urgent with the rise of literalism and the infallibility of scripture interpretation which is surfacing. It is more important than ever to bring back some minds who are being driven away by platitudes and by requirements for literal interpretation, which creationism and dispensationalism demand as signs of faith. This drives many thinking people away from the church, and the emphasis on death and some other world in eternity distracts people from finding real faith meaning for life in this world. We have taken on a Santa Claus mentality that says, "You better watch out. You better not cry. You better not pout. I'm telling you why. Jesus Christ is coming to town. He sees you when you're sleeping. He knows if you're awake. He knows if you've been bad or good, so be good for goodness sake." Jesus said it was wrong to place millstones around the necks of children, allowing them to drown in a sea of doubt and uncertainty. Paul says, "It is time to put away childish things." I decided the time had come to put down in writing some basic answers to faith questions that have come to my attention through the years, and this little book is my humble contribution on the face of this dilemma.

INTRODUCTION

There are many religions in the world, with reality and validity in every one of them. A common thread in all is a search for meaning in existence. This search for good life experiences takes place in a variety of venues. Primitive religions were based upon the belief that people were dependent upon powers and forces in their immediate environment, and were an attempt to relate to supernatural powers, which they believed could affect their daily lives through making crops grow, or through making domestic animals healthy and fertile so they would produce offspring to continue the species, enabling their owners to survive and bringing them wealth and security. In a way, this element remains in most modern religions.

We see this still in the religions of Africa, India, Iran, the Arab world, the Middle East, China, Japan, and other Asian countries. In India, Hinduism's mythology brought many gods into being, which affected life and eventually led people to deny worldliness. Out of this the ascetic lifestyle evolved in Jainism. Buddhism moved from a commonsense view of the world to denial of worldly things. Optimism and hope emerged in later Buddhism. Hinduism put its stamp on the social structure of India. Then the Sikhs welcomed other religions to join them, bringing into being the modern syncretism of the Hindu religion.

In China, Taoism and Confucianism were optimistic and humanistic, with a moral code. Shinto was Japanese patriotism become religious. Persian Zoroastrianism developed a religion of ethical dualism. In the Arabian culture, Muhammad's teachings in the Koran merged with Middle Eastern cultural traditions and evolved into Islam. Also in the Middle East, Judaism focused on one tribal God, Yahweh, viewed as Creator and lord of history and social behavior, a covenant God. Jesus emerged from Hebrew history, genealogy, and literature as prophet and teacher. Then the apostle Paul systematized a New Covenant for the Hebrews, and Christianity was formed. All of these religions were about how spiritual forces from Gods above or people's spirit within helped provide meaning for existence and coping mechanisms for living.

An ethical component for human behavior is embedded in the variety of religious writings. Consider the written words of what we call the Golden Rule. Christianity says, "In everything, do to others as you would have them do to you." Islam says, "No one of you is a believer until he loves for his brother what he loves for himself." Taoism says, "Regard your neighbor's gain as your own gain and regard your neighbor's loss as your own loss." Zoroastrianism says, "That nature only is good when it shall not do unto another whatever is not good for its own self." Buddhism says, "In five ways should a clansman minister to his friends and families—by generosity, courtesy, and benevolence, by treating them as he treats himself, and by being as good as his word." Hinduism says, "Men gifted with intelligence should always treat others as they themselves wish to be treated." Jainism says, "In happiness and suffering, in joy and grief, we should regard all creatures as we regard our own self." Sikhism says, "As you deem yourself so deem others. Then you shall become a partner in heaven." Judaism says, "You shall love your neighbor as yourself." Even atheism, which claims that God does not exist, and agnosticism, which claims that you cannot know if God exists or not, have ethical components. In these views, materialism is put in the place of God, but ethics akin to religious ethics still emerge. These are the ethics of secular humanism. Overall, to be human seems to require caring for others.

Common themes run through the stories and myths of the various religions. They include creation stories, flood stories and covenants, tales of the judgment of the gods, serpents representing evil, life and death, new birth or resurrection and redemption. These are reflections of life experiences, and what it is all about is getting the messages from the stories, myths, and metaphors that have emerged in the various religious cultures. The forces at work in creating such stories and myths seem to be a universal part of human nature in response to the environment. The purpose of going back to such stories and myths is to enrich the lives of people by conveying the religious messages. All religions have time-tested value, and have been a help to various peoples of the world. If they were of no help to people they would not have come into being, or would have long ago ceased to provide any meaning or message for existence, and would have disappeared from the culture and belief systems of earth's peoples.

My understanding of the world's religions and evaluative worldviews has been shaped by my upbringing and has been limited on the basis of my understanding of the world and my place in it. In addition, my experience led me into the calling of pastor in Presbyterian churches, where I have been confronted by real people and their search for meaning. This is the point where my thoughts begin. I have long felt a need for more to be said in the area of making sense for today of the Christian faith in the modern world, as it has been meaningful and helpful to me throughout the years. Religions and denominational interpretations are manifold, and many seem so certain of their beliefs that they feel it proper to persuade or even force others to agree with their particular views. I feel that I have some insights into what enlightened Christianity has to offer to the world, in contrast to what extremists and fundamentalists have been proclaiming and demanding. I want to share my understanding as a reality religious faith people can accept, and possibly be helped by, in the framework of the realities of the modern scientific and educated world. It is not an attempt to press anything on anyone already satisfied with his or her religious beliefs. It is for any who want help discovering a faith, which does provide meaning and enjoyment of life without checking their mind at the entrance of a faith worldview. This is an examination of the faith, which the Biblical literature's stories, myths, and metaphors present to us, through the avenue of questions asked of me about the Bible, and the Christian faith through the years answered in the light of the basic knowledge accepted in the twenty-first century of the Common Era.

BEGINNING QUESTIONS

WHERE AND HOW DO I BEGIN TO FIND A RELIGION THAT IS REAL TODAY?

I begin with generally accepted scientific reality. In the distant past, according to physicists, a big bang originated, and began the expanding universe. Nuclear fusion powered suns and formed galaxies. Around these suns gaseous and solid matter orbited. One such collection of matter formed the earth, and as time passed the planet we live on developed from the mass of molten materials, forming a crust, which collected by force of gravity an atmosphere and moisture. In primeval pools of moisture, primitive euglena-type cells formed the first primitive life on Earth. These evolved by survival of the fittest to form the sea creatures, which in their biological history eventually became amphibious and ventured onto the land. Land life became more complex, and over four billion years humans evolved from primitive mammals, along with other life forms in Africa. Today humans dominate the world and all of its complex life forms.

My religious tradition brings me to the literature we now know as the Bible, literature collected and written down some three thousand years ago. This is where I begin. The first eleven chapters of Genesis are a mixture of priestly poetry, mythology, bits of tradition, racial history, and theological reflection, giving us the Hebrew version of their origins, along with the belief that God was behind the creative process that enabled humans to multiply and disburse over the then known world.

It has much in common with similar mythology of other cultures, such as the Sumerian flood stories. In the promise made to Noah in the Biblical story after the flood subsided, you have the beginnings of what is known as covenant theology, the foundation of Biblical writing. "God said, 'This is the sign that I make between me and you and every living creature . . . I have set my bow in the clouds and it shall be a sign of the covenant between me and the earth . . . and the waters shall never again become a flood to destroy all flesh." (Genesis 9:12–15)

The Bible starts with the book called Genesis, meaning beginning. The first words in it are the convictions of the Hebrew priests. "In the beginning when God created the heavens and the earth, the earth was a formless void and darkness covered the face of the deep, while a wind from God swept over the face of the waters." (Genesis 1:1–2) Then follow the seven days of creation in the text. The Hebrew priest used seven days to reinforce Sabbath observance and the belief that God was behind, and in the midst of, the creative process. It is a theological poem never intended by the gatherer of the writings to be a scientific description of development of life on the planet. Arguments over creationism versus evolution trivialize the profound insights presented through the Biblical stories. The belief being set forth in them is that there is a creator-god who, by the wind of the spirit, brought forth the world, and the life upon it. Yahweh, the Hebrew name for God, roughly translated, means "the one who causes to be." Controversy over such things as seven days or eons and the reality of Adam and Eve are meaningless, and confuse the seeker. "Adam" and "Eve" are generic words meaning "mankind" and "mother of all living," intended to be seen not as individual people but as representative of all humankind, along with the recognition that a God of the universe was involved in the creation process and the evolution of all life on the planet. The Adam and Eve garden story is a timeless allegorical description of human selfishness and alienation or sin.

Genesis 12-50, which follow, are a mixture of legend, myth, and history that tell the particular ancestral story of the Middle Eastern people known as the Hebrews. The story of Abram's migration from the Chaldean city of Ur to Canaan is the foundation of the covenant theology noted in the Noah story, and his descendants are the covenant people. The children of Jacob become the twelve tribes of Israel; their sojourn to Egypt and later departure, or Exodus, from there form the framework for Hebrew history. In Chapter 7 of Genesis, the story is told of Jacob's name change to Ish-ra-el, meaning Son of God. From here on, the Bible becomes the story of the children of Israel.

The Bible is made up of two parts, the Old Covenant or Testament and the New Covenant or Testament. The words of the old covenant are found in Genesis 12:1–3, "Now the Lord said to Abram, 'Go from your country and your kindred and your father's house to the land that I will show you. And I will make of you a great nation and I will bless you, and make your name great, so that you will be a blessing. I will bless those who bless you and him who curses you I will curse; and in you all the families of the earth shall be blessed.'"

WHAT DO THE MANY BOOKS IN THE BIBLE TELL US?

The Old Testament books are the collected literature of the descendents of Abram, put in written form a thousand years after the life of Abram, gleaned from the campfire ancestral hero tales of the ancestors. The book of Genesis is a collection of myth, poetry, history, and legend, telling the story of the Creator's steadfast love in spite of the rebellions of the

Hebrew people, which culminates in the establishment of the covenant to restore humankind. Exodus tells of the faithfulness of God, the creator, to the covenant shown through the deliverance of Abram's Hebrew descendents from slavery in Egypt. Leviticus is made up of laws worked out to govern the Hebrew people and maintain their covenant relationship. Numbers is the census organizing the Hebrews to prepare them for covenant living. Deuteronomy is rediscovery of a legal interpretation of the covenant and directions for living under it. This much of the Bible is known as the Pentateuch and is the sacred Torah of Judaism.

Joshua is a story of Hebrew conquest to gain a land for covenant living. Judges is the story of God's faithfulness in delivering a rebellion-prone people from oppression through charismatic leaders called judges. I–II Samuel tells of a kingdom established under the leadership of Samuel, Saul, and David. I–II Kings describes the breakdown of the kingdom and the captivity in Babylon when the people forgot the covenant. I–II Chonicles is a different writer's view of the kingdom and its breakdown, and Ezra and Nehemiah center on the return of the Hebrews from captivity in Babylon and the attempt to reestablish the covenant and covenant living. Ruth is a story written during a time of national pride, pointing out Yahweh's use of a non-Hebrew in the period of the Judges to establish the line of King David, and Esther is a story of God's care of the Hebrews in exile. Job is a Hebrew play, considering the problem of why the righteous suffer.

Psalms is a collection of the Hebrew people's devotional literature, and Proverbs a collection of Hebrew wisdom literature. Ecclesiastes is a poetic questioning of the type of wisdom literature in Proverbs. Song of Songs is love poetry of the day, interpreted as related to God and his people. Lamentations are poems of sorrow and lament over the destruction of Jerusalem when the Hebrews became exiles in Babylon. Jonah is a humorous, mythical, and imaginary story written during a time of excessive Hebrew nationalism, telling of a prophet who tried to run away from God's call to help some non-Hebrews.

The books that follow are the writings of the Covenant nation's men of insight known as Prophets. These were not soothsayers or fortunetellers who foretell events in the future but insightful persons with deep faith and conviction who made thoughtful observations on the life and affairs of their day and sought to influence their leaders and contemporaries. Isaiah contains words of warning to the covenant nation, Judah, and the city of Jerusalem before the Assyrian conquest of the nation of Israel. In the last part, from Chapter 40 on, a different person offers words of encouragement and hope during the exile in Babylon. Jeremiah is made up of admonitions to the covenant nation of Judah just before and during the captivity by Babylon, and is a record of many events of the time. Ezekiel has visions and thoughts of a Hebrew Priest to reawaken and encourage the covenant people while in exile. Daniel interprets the late history of the covenant people with stories and visions from exile and points out that even in their time of persecution God still rules and his purposes will finally be fulfilled. Hosea is a pleading with the nation of Israel before its captivity by Assyria to return to the covenant God. Joel is a warning to Judah and the city of Jerusalem at the time of a locust plague. Amos is warnings to the nation Israel before its destruction and captivity by Syria. Obadiah contains threats to the nation of Edom for its mistreatment of the covenant nation of Judah when the people were taken into exile. Micah warns both Israel and Judah before the Syrian captivity of the nation Israel. Nahum has words of warning to the city of

Nineveh in Syria in its time of power. Habbakuk also warns, but in addition has words of faith before the captivity of Judah by Babylon. Zephaniah gives warnings to Judah, but with a note of hope before its captivity. Haggai offers guidance to Zerubbabel, Governor of Judah at the end of the Babylonian exile. Zechariah cautions and instills hope to the covenant people returning from exile in Babylon, and Malachi warns and admonishes the covenant people following the exile.

This briefly summarizes the literature that makes up the sixty-six books of the Old Testament. In them can be found timeless meaningful messages related to daily life when they are read as the historical and mythological literature they originally were. They are of value in and of themselves, and important for sound Biblical understanding. They are not replaced by the New Testament, nor are they meant to foretell what happens in it. They are the foundation stones on which the New Testament stories, events, and ideas are built, and are essential for sound interpretation and understanding of it and the total Biblical message.

In the New Testament or Covenant, Mark, Matthew, and John are collections and condensations of the early church's view of the events, life, ministry, and teachings of Jesus through witnesses and his preaching. These, along with Luke, are known as the Gospels, the Good News of and about Jesus.

Luke and Acts are grouped together because they are by the same writer and are like two volumes based on one continuous story. In this, we find a repeat of the Jesus story from a different perspective, plus a history of the formation and growth of the early church. The writings that follow are largely letters over a period of time addressed to leaders and people, the believers or followers of Jesus who made up the young church gatherings of believers congregating together in cities around Asia Minor. They became known as Christians. The letters were addressed to Romans, Corinthians, Galatians, Ephesians, Philippians, Colossians, and Thessalonians, as well some individuals, Timothy, Titus, and Philemon. The book titled as Hebrews is an anonymous letter dealing with the superiority of Christianity over Judaism, and James is a reminder to Christians as to how they should live, attributed to James, the brother of Jesus, but probably written later by someone claiming his authority. The message is always more important than the person who wrote it. I–II Peter are letters of support and encouragement to Christians undergoing persecution for their faith. Peter, the disciple, was probably not the actual writer, since it came from a later time in the development of the church. I–II John are letters admonishing Christians to love and care for one another and III John is a letter of encouragement to an individual named Gaius. Jude is a letter against false teachers and the Revelation to John is the New Testament counterpart to the Old Testament book of Daniel, with pictures and poetic imagery which proclaims, as Daniel does, that in times of persecution of the faithful, God is still present first, last, and always. People have many questions related to this book, and I will try to help with these at a later point.

This collection of Old and New Covenant history is known as the Holy Bible. The word "holy" means "set apart." This collection serves as the foundation for all Judeo-Christian thought and convictions as read, translated, preached, taught, and interpreted down through the years.

WHAT ARE THE KEY NEW TESTAMENT SCRIPTURES?

A critical premise of the New Testament or Covenant is that Jesus is the word of God, Yahweh, made flesh. "And the word became flesh and lived among us full of grace and truth. The law, indeed was given through Moses, grace and truth came through Jesus Christ." (John 1:14–17) Then, "So if anyone is in Christ, there is a new creation: everything old has passed away; see everything has become new! All this is from God, who reconciled us to himself through Christ, and has given us the ministry of reconciliation; that is, in Christ God was reconciling the world to himself, not counting their trespasses against them, entrusting the message of reconciliation to us so we are ambassadors for Christ." (II Corinthians 5:17–19) Next, "There is no longer Jew or Greek, there is no longer slave or free, there is no longer male or female, for all of you are one in Christ Jesus. And if you belong to Christ, then you are Abraham's offspring, heirs according to the promise." (Galatians 3:38–39 and Romans 3:23–25a.) "For there is no distinction, since all have sinned and fall short of the Glory of God, they are now justified by his grace as a gift, through the redemption that is in Christ Jesus, whom God put forward as sacrifice and atonement by his blood effective through faith." I consider these to be the salient messages of the New Testament or New Covenant and basic to an understanding of the faith, as a continuation of the Old Covenant made to Abraham. It is not about rules and our obedience to them, but rather about the grace of God who loves us steadfastly and has intervened in history to show this love, and our grateful response to this.

OTHER BIBLICAL QUESTIONS

HOW DID GOD MAKE PEOPLE BEFORE HE WAS BORN?

This important question came to my attention from a young child and reveals a confusion coming from mixing up Jesus and God, or equating them. Historical perspective is difficult for a child, and adults make the same error when they turn Jesus into God in their thoughts. The initial words of Genesis point out that God's spirit was sweeping over the watery chaos. God was at the world's beginning, creating and fashioning order out of chaos. God, according to the Hebrew priest who wrote the creation poem in Genesis, was involved in the creation process, which culminated in humanity. The priest thought that the earth was flat and that the world had three levels: first, the waters beneath and around the earth. Second, the middle level of the earth itself, and third, the sky dome with the waters above, and the sun and the moon and the stars. You could dig into the earth for water, or walk until you came upon it in a river or sea. Water also came from the sky dome when the windows of the heavens opened dripping rain. This beautifully descriptive poem, limited by the science of the day, painted the picture within a seven-day process, with six days for work, and the seventh for worship and rest. The priest who wrote the creation account had a vested interest in the Sabbath worship. After God's inspired leaders failed to communicate the covenant faith, the Word that had inspired the leaders was made flesh in Jesus. Jesus was a particular human being anointed or called to make God personal. The word "Christ" means "anointed one." Jesus makes God tangible and personal for us, bringing him within reach. He communicates all that God is in human terms, making God's word more understandable and specific to people than just the words of charismatic leaders and spiritually sensitive prophets before him. Jesus, the anointed one, becomes a personal communication to humankind of all that God is.

HOW DO WE KNOW THERE IS A GOD?

To believe is to accept God as creator, redeemer, and sustainer of the universe and all its life. In the modern world, with the decline of superstitious beliefs, there are many who do not believe that there is a God. Sigmund Freud believed that the Judeo-Christian God was a psychological projection of the desire of people for a celestial father figure. He said, in effect, that people created gods out of their own needs to solve some of the problems of existence. (1) Charles Darwin, based on his study of living species in the world, believed that life evolved in a pattern of the survival-of-the-fittest changes in organisms over billions of years, and the geological record on earth supports that conclusion. The early Hebrew priests believed that the spirit of God, breathing on the primeval watery chaos on earth, produced life. Today, people of faith believe that a creator God was endemic to the process of evolution. An Intel Pentium computer chip, which makes it possible for me to type these words into my computer, did not just happen by accident. It was designed, built, and manufactured by people. People created the chip. It didn't just happen. Similarly, the earth as we experience it today and the universe around us didn't just happen. A creator shared in the process of evolution. Such a belief helps us grasp the orderliness of the universe.

A handful of printer's type tossed into the air does not fall into an intelligent sentence by chance. A sentence has to be created and written in the mind of a person to happen. Similarly, we believe that an orderly universe requires a creator involved in the process to make the complexities of the universe plausible. When we examine history and human experience, we can catch glimpses of God's spirit at work. The very existence of modern religions such as the Judeo-Christian faith testifies to the work of God, since it probably would not be sustained by chance or superstition alone. It is a way of viewing the eternal God in life as a foundation or premise of our existence as human beings, which can give meaning, purpose, and joy to our lives.

WHERE DOES JESUS FIT INTO THIS?

The various religions are based on different ideas of the nature and persona of the idea of God. Jesus is the personification of God. The idea of God was distant apart from Jesus. He brings God down to earth and accessible to humanity. Jesus of Nazareth, called the Christ, fits into the redemptive and sustaining role of God. "Christos," in Greek, means "the anointed ruler and expected savior." It is not his last name, but recognition of his role, his mission, his calling. Jesus was understood as having a redemptive role in Christian thought. He is the messiah, the savior, and the redeemer. He is the one who offers himself to make those who follow him worth something. He remakes lives, and can be understood as a valued redemption coupon offered to make his followers more than they could be without his life, work, and inspiration.

WHAT DOES IT MEAN TO BE SAVED?

The beginning of the answer to this question is another question. What are we saved from? We are saved from being limited, self-centered beings. I believe that a life of discipleship to Jesus enables us to overcome this natural tendency and find direction for our living, helping us to become our best selves. We are saved from purposeless, aimless living. Jesus saves us to find direction for our lives, becoming all that God created us to be. He saves us from a life of separation from God, providing continuing help in our ongoing relationship to God and others. We are freed from being self-absorbed and self-conscious. This is what sin is. It ruins our relationship to God and others and degrades our living. We are saved for fuller life. Salvation is not a promise of some better life in some future heaven. We are saved for life and living, not death and dying. We are saved for this life. "I come that you may have life and have it more abundantly." (John 10:10) To be saved is not just saying "Jesus is my Lord and Savior" to purchase a passport to a future heaven. Being saved, and in relation to God, others, and the world, is where we are now, in a day-to-day sense. To be saved enables us to overcome the corrupting power of self-centered living, freeing us to become authentic human beings. Jesus is a paradigm of authenticity for humanity, showing us the way, and saving us from selfishness. This is what it means to be saved.

WHAT IS THE MEANING OF THE GARDEN OF EDEN STORY?

This early myth is a Hebrew priest's explanation of the human condition. It is a story of human selfishness and rebellion. The man and woman dwelling in an idyllic garden were not satisfied with its limits, and wanted more. They desired to be like God, so they broke the boundaries of subservience to God by eating of the symbolic forbidden fruit, probably a pomegranate. (Apples don't grow in the Euphrates River area.) The innocence of people was replaced by self-will and self-centeredness. This is the definition of sin. It is not wrongdoing, or breaking the rules. These are byproducts of sin. Putting ourselves and our will in God's place, loving our selves more than loving God and other people are what throw our lives out of balance, leading to separation from God and others. The story of love losing its balance is the meaning and message of the Garden of Eden myth, and being cast out of the garden describes picturesquely the problem of humanity without God; this message is dealt with all through the Bible.

IS THE STORY OF NOAH AND THE ARK TRUE?

This is another child's question. Every once in a while, an article appears in the paper about someone searching for the archeological remains of Noah's Ark. Sophisticated archaeologists don't search for evidence of past arks because they know the story comes from a period in history where people were looking back into their unrecorded past to discern their early origins. It is an epic myth about Noah, a folk hero. Floods were common in the Tigris-Euphrates river basin, and tales about an especially big one in the past were also common. This one tells of the opening of the windows of the heavens and the releasing of the subterranean waters for the cosmic destruction of humankind. The Sumerians and other ancient cultures had similar flood stories, but the point of this Hebrew story was that after God's judgment through the forces of nature comes God's forgiveness and the promise that God will never again destroy wayward humankind. The rainbow is depicted as the sign of this promise and an early witness to the idea of the grace of God. Is the story true? The truth is in the point that the story makes, not in the literal historical accuracy of an actual boat four hundred and fifty by seventy-five by forty-five feet long, containing two each of all the animals of the earth, for forty days and forty nights. The truth is in the story's meaning and message, not the facts. There is history in the ancestry and the genealogy. The sons of Noah were Shem, Ham, and Japheth. Shem was the early ancestor, the forefather of the Semitic Hebrew peoples who were the Moabites, Edomites, and Israelites. Ham was the progenitor, the forefather, of the peoples of the Egyptian area, and Japheth those who inhabited Asia Minor. History is woven into the myths and legends, the stories of the people, but the larger meanings are why they are passed on and remembered.

DID A LARGE FISH REALLY SWALLOW JONAH?

There is a Jonah mentioned in II Kings 14:25 as a servant of King Jeroboam, "Jonah son of Amatti, the prophet who was from Gath-hepher," but the iconic story in the Biblical book of Jonah is unrelated to this King's Court servant prophet. It is a story told during a period of intense Jewish nationalism and sectarian exclusivism. The Jonah in it is told to go at once to Nineveh, a land hostile to Israel, and cry out against it, but Jonah boards a boat sailing in the opposite direction. When a storm at sea almost capsizes the boat, the sailors cast lots to see who aboard might be being punished by God's causing the storm. They blame Jonah and throw him overboard. A great fish swallows him, and after three days and three nights, the fish spits him out on shore, as close to Nineveh as the fish could swim. Jonah reluctantly proclaims that Nineveh in forty days will be overthrown unless they repent. The people listen, repent, and put on sackcloth and ashes to show their distress. Displeased that the Ninevites have responded to the prophecy, Jonah becomes angry, and goes off into the desert to sulk under the shade of a bush. The bush dies, and the hot wind blows, and Jonah asks that he too might die, and the story has God say: "You are concerned bout the bush, for which you did not labor and which you did not grow. It came into being in a night and perished in a night. Should I not be concerned about Nineveh, that great City, in which there are more than a hundred and twenty thousand persons who do not know their right hand from their left, and also many animals?" That question penned by the writer holds the key to the whole story. The great fish and bush are literary devices used to make the profound point that God, Yahweh, cares not only for the Hebrews but also for all people, and even their animals. Biblical literature uses myth and metaphor to provide meaning. This fascinating little story can help us in reading much of the Bible. Recognize that myth and metaphor are probable in the text and read it for meaning. These are the three M's of Biblical interpretation for both the Old and the New Testament. Ask yourself as you read: "What does this story incident mean in its context for me in my life now?" As you read the Bible, think three M's: myth, metaphor, and meaning, and then you can perceive and understand the fourth M, the message intended for your own personal life.

WHAT IS A MYTH AND WHAT IS A METAPHOR?

Myths are traditional stories often related to historical events concerned with gods and legendary heroes of a people. They are a way of communicating important beliefs and understandings of the people who pass them down. Biblical myths are meaningful and important messages presented in this form. Their truth lies in the meaning and the message they convey, not in their historical reality.

A metaphor is a figure of speech using words or phrases where one kind of object or idea is used in place of another to suggest the likeness or analogy between them. The Biblical material is full of metaphors to help people get the messages and literal reading can often lead to missing the meaning or message, which is the really important part.

IS THE BIBLE ABOUT MORALS AND ETHICS?

We tend to read the Bible as primarily a rulebook and guide for behavior. The behavior or moral guide is found in the Prophetic writings of the Old Covenant. God's love for his people is steadfast. The Hebrew word for steadfast love is "Hesed." It is scattered through the Old Covenant literature, at least a hundred and seventy-one times by my count. It is clear that this steadfast love of God is to be responded to with gratitude. It is in the Hebrew law. "Hear, O Israel: The Lord is our God, the Lord alone. You shall love the Lord your God with all your heart and with all your soul and with all your might. Keep these words that I am commanding you today in your heart. Recite them to your children and talk about them when you are at home and when you are away. When you lie down and when you rise." (Deuteronomy 6:4–5) Gratitude to God is the foundation of ethics. It is expressed through our loving and just dealings with others. The Prophet Micah said, "He has told you, O mortal what is good; and what does the Lord require of you but to do justice and love kindness and to walk humbly with your God." (Micah 6:8)

This same message is reiterated in the New Covenant Literature. "One of the scribes came near and heard them disputing with one another, and seeing that he answered them well, he asked him, 'Teacher, which commandment is the greatest?' Jesus answered, 'The first is, 'Hear O Israel: The Lord our God, the Lord is one; you shall love the Lord your God with all your heart, and with all your soul and with all your mind, and with all your strength.' The second is this. 'You shall love your neighbor as yourself.' There is no commandment greater than these. (Mark 12:28–31) Jesus added to the Old Covenant credo "You shall love your neighbor as yourself."

Love for God and others is the main ethical and moral thrust of the Biblical faith and translates into social justice for all, especially the poor and needy. This is the primary message Judaism and Christianity have been trying to communicate to their constituency and the world all through history. The word "love" occurs five hundred and eighty-four times in the Bible. The Hebrew word in the Old Testament is "Hesed," standing for the steadfast love of God for people. The New Testament Greek words for love are "Eros," physical love, "Philos," friendship love, and "Agape," unconditional love. This is similar to the old Testament Hebrew word "Hesed," in the old Testament, standing for the steadfast love of God for people. This love trumps all other rules in the Biblical literature.

In the present-day church there is an overemphasis on sexuality, male and female marriage partnerships, anti-homosexual and anti-abortion concerns. The basic moral and ethical message is clearly "Love God and others." The theme of social justice occurs a hundred and sixty-five times in the Biblical literature, and concern for the poor two hundred and four times. The subject of sodomy is mentioned only four times, in Liviticus 18:22 & 20:13, I Corinthians 6:9, and I Timothy 1:10, and abortion is not mentioned at all. This majoring in minor matters distorts and distracts from the important message.

IS THE BIBLE TRUE?

Spoken and written words are instruments of communication. God communicates through people affected by and inspired by God. Biblical writings are limited, as are other writings by the understanding and worldview of the people who wrote them. When people were telling the stories, or putting their thoughts into words, they believed that the world was flat, and their understanding of it was limited to the Near East. They didn't have or need the modern advantages of catalogued scientific knowledge. In Joshua 10:12–13: "On the day when the Lord gave the Amorites over to the Israelites Joshua spoke to the Lord; and he said in the sight of Israel. 'Sun stand still at Gibeon, and Moon in the valley of Aijalon' and the sun stood still and the moon stopped until the nation took vengeance on their enemies." The Israelites believed that their God, Yahweh, fought with them against their enemies, and had no knowledge of what the consequences of such an action would have on planet earth or the celestial moon. They did not know they were on a spherical planet and that the interruption of the sun and earth's inertia and massive resulting shifts in the tectonic plates of the earth would have caused earthquakes far more devastating than the battle they were waging. They thought they lived on a large flat plate floating on water, and the literalism of their mythology spared them from these concerns. This did not detract from their faith in God as the controller of their destiny. The people who formed the Hebrew mythology which became the holy life story of the work of God in their midst were human beings with human limits, but still an inspired people enabling them to be a vehicle for communication of God's truths to the peoples of the earth.

WHAT DOES IT MEAN TO SAY THE BIBLE IS THE WORD OF GOD?

To say the Bible is the Word of God is not to say it is the "words" of God. It is the words of people, limited by mythology and ignorance. Through the lives and experiences of this set-apart people, descended from Abraham, an insightful literature was imparted which still reaches us. Translation and interpretation, also part of the tools used by God, bring these truths down through the ages. Jesus is the Word made flesh. He is the humanization of the words of the prophets and the forefathers, the embodiment of the written and spoken word picked up by others and communicated again through spoken and written words.

HOW DO THE STORIES OF THE OLD TESTAMENT RELATE MEANINGFULLY TO MODERN LIFE?

The covenant myths and stories of the Old Testament are many and varied. Some are legendary accounts of the early fathers of the tribes of Israel. The time span is from Abraham, two millennia before the Common Era, to about fifteen hundred years before the Common Era. They are historical sketches from Israel's past told over and over because they made contributions to their history or had special significance to the Hebrews. Non-historical stories and myths, which made a social or theological point to their community, were also collected. Job, for example, is a Hebrew play, which dealt with the question "Why do the righteous and upright suffer?" Jonah's story, cited before, dealt with the ethnocentrism of the Hebrews and the problem this brought to authentic life under God's covenant with his people, and points up that God cares about people other than the Hebrew people. Psalms is the Hebrew hymnbook. Ecclesiastes is Hebrew wisdom literature comparable to Benjamin Franklin's *Poor Richard's Almanac*. Such literature bears on modern life because it comes from a people attempting to live in relationship with God, just as we are doing today as contemporary people of God. Society has progressed and continues to change at an accelerating pace, but human beings of three thousand years ago are of the same basic nature as contemporary human beings. Hence many of the experiences and insights still speak to the human condition today. The Hebrew experience is still of help, because it is the experience of a people sensitive to the spirit of God in their midst. These people were set apart as God's chosen method for communicating to the world. The same God who spoke then speaks today through the understandings and experiences of people. Again, examine the mythical story, consider the metaphor, and reflect on the meaning, and the message for you will emerge in a flash of insight.

WAS JESUS ACTUALLY BORN OF A VIRGIN?

We have to understand this in terms of the times. At the time Jesus was born, those of great power and influence were viewed as special people sent by the Gods. The Caesars of Rome were consolidating their power and earning loyalty by claiming divine origins. Leaders often claimed mythological "virgin births." By the time the gospels of Matthew and Luke were collected and organized by the church, Jesus had become important to the fledgling followers of the way of Jesus. He was given authority and status in their lives in the same way as the contemporary rulers of the day were given mythological status by ascribing virgin births to them. The Greek Gospel writer, Luke, gave that same status to Jesus in the mythological birth story of his origins. He was descended, according to the genealogy of the Hebrews, from the line of David, the greatest king of Israel, so the logic here was clear. He was their ruler and deserves this honor as their ruler. Only Luke, among the Gospel writers, referred to Jesus being born of a virgin, imposing this Grecian thought in his gospel narrative. This was a theological point rather than an analysis of a physiological premise of an absence of impregnation. The early Roman Catholic Church constructed a complex pattern of reasoning to maintain the purity of Mary, as it became important in their theology. They claimed that Jesus had no brothers or sisters, even though they were specifically referred to and named in the New Testament stories. The logic to establish the role of Mary as the mother of God, and her sexual purity, which made Jesus the only Son of God in the thinking of the early church, needs demythologizing. Avoid focusing on the details and accuracy of the myth or metaphor, and concentrate on the theological meaning. The writer of the gospel of John called Jesus the Word of God made flesh. The theological meaning is that Jesus was sent by and chosen by God to endear our understanding of God's word to us in a personal and tangible way. God was in Jesus, Mary's child, sent to deepen our understanding of God and God's way and will for us, not as a biological matter but a theological one.

HOW DO WE UNDERSTAND AND INTERPRET JESUS'S MIRACLES?

The new Covenant Literature abounds in events that go beyond the normal and regular events of living. We call these miracles. How do we account for them? Is Jesus a miracle worker? Water is turned into wine at a wedding feast. Jesus is tempted to turn stones into bread, to satisfy his hunger. Five thousand are fed with a few loaves and fishes. A man so deranged that he has been banished from the town to the

Gerasene shore of the Sea of Galilee is healed. Ten banished lepers are healed. All of these have the characteristic of deviation from present realities, and are unexplainable events not in conformity with modern understandings of reality. They have something in common with the account of the captive Israelites fleeing across the sea from Pharaoh's pursuing soldiers. One version of what brought about the miracle of deliverance (Exodus 14:21–30) was the rising of a wall of water on the left and a wall of water on the right with dry land between when Moses raised his arms, and the miring down of the Chariots and marching soldiers, as soon as the waters returned to normal depth. The other version in Exodus was that with the raising of Moses's arms a strong east wind blew all night, making the waters shallower in the Reed Sea so the fleeing Israelites could wade through, but not shallow enough for the chariot wheels or heavily armored soldiers to make it; when the wind ceased, the water returned to normal levels, drowning those bogged down. The myths were different since they are a blending together of the versions of two different writers, but the meaning was the same. God, Yahweh, had led the people to freedom.

Similar treatment of the myths of the New Testament can lead eventually to their meaning, once they are demythologized. In John 2:1–11 water was turned to wine by Jesus upon his mother Mary's mention of the predicament of the social embarrassment of the host. The water made wine was a departure from custom, since the best wine was served last rather than first. This meant that Jesus, in the minds of the early church preachers, had unusual gifts. When Jesus was seeking to discern the nature of his ministry in the wilderness temptation story found in Matthew 4:1–11, turning stones into bread was one of his considerations, and leaping off the temple pinnacle to prove his uniqueness was another. The third was to take over and rule the world, but as Jesus considered the course his ministry was to take, he chose not to focus on being a miracle worker but on meeting the spiritual needs of people. The feeding of the five thousand with the five loaves and two fish (John 6:9) can be understood in the example of the young boy's willingness to share what he had. This led others to follow suit so there was enough for all as others shared, and can be interpreted as a lesson in sharing. The healing of the Gerasene demoniac (Mark 5:1–20) came about because of Jesus's counsel and interest in restoring wholeness to the man. When he expressed his gratitude, Jesus sent him home to tell others how his personality, body, mind, and spirit were restored. In the story of the healing of the ten lepers (Luke 17:11–19), ten were cured, and sent to the priest, but only one, a Samaritan, came back to thank Jesus for what he had done and was then more fully healed. This was a lesson in gratitude, but it also points up that the neighboring, foreign Samaritans were also of concern to God.

Demythologize the healing myths and metaphors to get the meaning of the miracles. Read all miracle stories in the Biblical literature for personal meaning for the living of your life, not as evidence of supernatural powers of God or Jesus or his disciples. In this way, you will get to the heart of it to discover more meaning for your own personal life and existence.

WHAT ABOUT PARABLES?

A parable is a short story about first-century living, used to illustrate a moral attitude or a religious principle. They are timely, everyday stories, which serve as illustrations that can help us understand our present relationship to God and one another, as do other ancient myths and metaphors. The meaning of what is being illustrated is the important part.

The parable of the Generous Employer in Matthew 20:1–16 is a good example. Jesus tells of a landowner who needs workers for his vineyard, and goes to the town square, something like a temporary workers' employment office, and hires all of the hands he could find. This is early in the morning and he agrees to pay them a denarius, the going daily wage rate. Three hours later, about nine o'clock, still needing workers, he goes back and hires some more workers, the late risers, at what he calls the "right" wage. At noon and at three in the afternoon he hires more, and five o'clock finds him again in the town square as the shadows lengthen, where a few men still wait disconsolately for work. He appraises them with a quick glance. Are they loafers, or just unemployed for the day? He asks them, "Why are you idle?" They reply, "Because nobody has hired us," and his instruction is, "You too go to my vineyard." The end of the workday comes, and the vineyard owner pays all of the workers the same amount, one denarius. Those who have worked from early sunrise through the heat of the day are paid exactly the same as those who have worked only an hour in the evening before sunset, and, to make matters worse, those who were hired last are paid first. In the story, the early workers grumble, and the vineyard owner says to one of those who complains, "Friend, I am doing you no wrong. Did you not agree with me for the usual daily wage? Take what belongs to you and go. I choose to give to the last the same as I gave to you. Am I not allowed to do what I choose with what belongs to me? Or are you envious because I am generous?" At the end of the story Jesus states, "So the last will be first and the first will be last."

The meaning and message of this story Jesus tells is not obvious on the surface. It seems unfair to those of us who would probably find ourselves among the grumbling day laborers. Two important thoughts emerge from this parable, on the nature of the kingdom of God. If God is like this generous employer, God is gracious, rewarding us with his mercy and acceptance despite our faults and weaknesses, and no matter how long or hard we work to earn our relationship to God. Meaning for life and work do not consist of punching the time clock and putting in time for a paycheck or reward at the end of the day. There is reward to be found in living life joyfully and usefully in relation to God and others. The joy is in the life and labor, not the reward at the end of the day. In addition, the parable implies that all are honored and rewarded equally. This is a reversal of what we tend to think: that the first should receive more. The parable points out that all will be honored and rewarded, even though some think the last aren't worth as much. Jesus sums up the story with, "The last will be first and the first last." This is to say equal payment of all, or all will be first. Through this simple story, Jesus makes the profound point that God's grace and mercy are not a reward but a gift, equally available to all, and we need not grumble but, rather, be enthusiastically grateful.

WHAT IS BEING BORN AGAIN?

The first birth obviously takes place when we are thrust from our mother's womb. The second birth is when we become aware of the significance of our relationship to God. We experience a spiritual birth. This is what Jesus talked to Nicodemus, the religious Hebrew Pharisee, about in John 3:1–17. Nicodemus took him literally and found it difficult to understand what it meant to be "born from above." Thinking literally gave him trouble understanding this core Christian belief that profoundly changes people's lives. It has to do with moving from self-centeredness to God awareness that leads to a new understanding of the relationship one has to God and others. It is an awakening and awareness of the significance and meaning of God, and involves a new way of looking at one's self and life. This is such a radical change it can be looked upon as a second birth. This is a gradual growing process, not a one time event. We continue to be born from above throughout life.

THEOLOGICAL THOUGHT QUESTIONS

WHY DO WE HAVE TO DIE?

All biological organisms—microbe, plant, and animal—begin life, are born, grow to maturity, and continue their existence by growing or birthing new organisms. People are one of these life forms. We, like all other life forms, are born, mature, reproduce, and die. The human species has a great deal of difficulty in sharing in this universal mortality of organisms and species. This is especially offensive when we apply it to our own existence. In spite of the observable facts of life and death, we have conjectured and created many theories, which lead us to believe that we continue existence in some form or another after physical death. Among these is the Hindu belief that we are reincarnated into another life form. Egyptians, when they committed the remains of a Pharaoh in a pyramid, included items to contribute to the comfort of the deceased ruler in another life. Muslim suicide bombers are told that they will have a harem of virgins in their afterlife. Native Americans had hopes of a happy hunting ground after death. Jesus's disciples reported him saying, "In my Father's house there are many dwelling places. If it were not so, would I have told you that I go to prepare a place for you?" (John 14:2) General belief assumes there is an afterlife place where we meet again with loved ones who await our deaths so we can all be reunited and see one another again. The more difficult living conditions are in present life experiences, the more apt we are to take hold of such conjecture. Afterlife talk and concern is part of religious mythology, but is often quite different from our stereotypes.

Biblical literature substantiates that God's care, which we have experienced in our faith relationships in life, continues through and after death. I asked Dr. Robert Wright, who had dedicated his life to being a Presbyterian medical missionary in Iran, "What is death?" and his answer was, "I believe it is like a deep sleep," and implied that there would be no consciousness of what was going on after death since the brain would simply cease to function. From a medical perspective, once we die we are like every other creature in the universe. At death, the brain ceases to function and our physical body becomes an empty shell. All God's creatures die, including humans, so for all practical purposes, we die and are simply no more.

Paul, the apostle, spoke of the perishable body putting on imperishability and the mortal body putting on immortality. (I Corinthians 15:53) Jesus implied that beyond this life, roles would be reversed. The rich man who received good things in life was in agony, and Lazarus, who experienced evil things in life, was comforted in death. (Luke 16:35) Jesus also said that the man who had seven wives on earth would not be married to any of them in "heaven." "For in the resurrection they neither marry or are given in marriage.' (Matthew 22:30) This implies that the renewal of human relationships, which people long for and cling to so tenaciously in an afterlife, are false hopes, and wishful thinking. Human relationships take place and are completed in life.

Most people, unless they are in the midst of extreme suffering or discomfort, do not want to die. In our various religions, we have envisioned some form of a heavenly afterlife. The writer of Ecclesiastes reflects on this. "I said in my heart with regard to human beings that God is testing them to show that they are but animals. For the fate of humans and the fate of animals is the same, as one dies so dies the other. They all have the same breath, and humans have no advantage over the animals; for all is vanity. All go to one place, all are from the dust, and all turn to dust again. Who knows whether the human spirit goes upward, and the spirit of animals goes downward to the earth? So I saw that there is nothing better than that all should enjoy their work, for that is their lot. Who can bring them to see what will be after them?" (Ecclesiastes 3:19–22)

The value of religion is for this life, not some next life. We can live this life confident that the relationship with God we discover in our earthly existence lives on, but that our human relationships are completed with death. This makes us aware of the importance of what we do with those relationships while we are alive. We can have ultimate trust and faith that God's care, which we have experienced in life, will continue beyond physical death in some appropriate way which we cannot now fully understand. Whatever is best for us and the world will occur at the time of our death. This probably means that our future involves simply expiring, to rest in peace, as is the case for all other life forms, from the greatest to the least, in this vast universe. Until the moment of our death, we mortals can, as the Ecclesiastes writer suggested, deal in life with the cards we are dealt, enjoying the game of life lived in relation to, and guided by, the eternal God. Death is viewed by those who experience such a rebirth of awareness to God and to others around them as a passageway to a type of third birth into the fullness of our relationship to God, not to other human beings. Whatever it is, we are in God's care.

WHAT ARE HEAVEN AND HELL?

The metaphors that Jesus used in reference to heaven and hell are descriptive of life experiences. The focus is not on place or location, but rather about the relationships that people have to God and one another in the here and now of living. Heaven is a relationship with the eternal God that begins in this life and continues beyond it. It is a depth relationship to God that takes place in the here and now and spills over into good relationships with others, bringing bliss into the present living of life. Heaven is being sensitive to God's will for your life, and the focus is on having good relationships with others. It is about having the right attitude toward life where you are in it. We have "One Foot in Heaven," as Hartzell Spence put it in the title of his novel. The good life begins here and now, not in the future after death. Heaven is not a physical place in the clouds above earth for everlasting bliss as repayment for good moral behavior or church membership. Heaven is a relationship with the eternal God which is real in life.

Hell is not a fiery place under the earth's surface, where you suffer for eternity, but the condition of being alienated and separated from God, family, friends and/or others. Jesus, in Mark 9:47–48, used the metaphor of being thrown into the valley of Hinnom or Gehenna, the garbage dump outside of Jerusalem where "maggots covered the decaying food, and trash continually burned." This illustrates graphically being identified with the castoffs of society, in outer darkness rather than in the light of God in life (Acts 26:18). The picture is of the outer darkness of an unlit garbage dump, rather than under the city's lights.

Heaven and hell are not places, but states of being not merely associated with death. In a spiritual sense, we are often there in our own present life experiences. Heaven is when we begin our relationship to God and carry this into our relationship to others. Our relationship with God enables us to find "heaven" and escape from "hell" in our present life. We need not focus on some unknown speculation regarding the future. Neither heaven nor hell is something related to the future. We can have in life, in the here and now, a depth relationship to God. Our relationship to the "heavenly Father" is available now. Lack of present relationship to God lessens the good experiences of our living in the present moments. Heaven is for life now, not something hoped for in some future existence. We then can rest assured that the God who cares for us in this life cares for us whatever the exact nature of life's ending may be.

WHAT DO WE MEAN BY THE KINGDOM OF GOD?

Jesus said in Luke 7:21, "The kingdom of God is among you," and in Mark 4:26–27, "The kingdom of God is as if someone would scatter seed upon the ground, and would sleep and rise, night and day, and the seed would sprout and grow he does not know how." It is not terminology for a heavenly place where God sits on a throne and rules the world. This points out that the growth of God's kingdom in the world is beyond human understanding or control. With the parable of the soils in Matthew 13:18–23, Jesus pointed out that the response to his message would be affected by the circumstances of human life. Mathew 13:32–33 is the parable of the mustard seed, where we see that though the kingdom has small beginnings it has the potential to grow in a startling way. The kingdom on earth is also subtle, Matthew 13:16–19, working like yeast, which in a small amount eventually leavens the whole loaf. In Matthew 13:44, he says that it has great value, like treasure hidden in a field, worth joyfully selling all you have to purchase it. The kingship of God is present now wherever there are people who are responding to God as ruler of their life. A kingdom involves subjects. We are part of the kingdom when we, by choice, respond to God's call and allow Jesus to model our lives. The growth of God's kingdom in the world is beyond human understanding or control, but it involves

God at work in this world with his subjects. As we relate to God, we become part of the kingdom of God. The realm of God's rule is not in some distant place but here on earth and in our daily lives.

WHAT DOES THE RESURRECTION OF JESUS MEAN TO US?

Jesus's disciples and followers were decimated and scattered after the Roman authorities, urged by the religious leaders who felt that he was competing with them, crucified him. Confusing and somewhat contradictory scripture myths of the post-death appearances of Jesus to his disciples emerged and were passed on. The gospel writer in Matthew 28:1–14 describes it as Pilate ordering soldiers to guard Jesus's tomb, and they rolled a stone to seal the entrance. After the Sabbath, Mary Magdalene and another Mary went to complete the burial preparation and found the tomb empty. Jesus appeared to them in the garden and said, "Do not be afraid. Go and tell my brothers to go to Galilee; where they will see me." The priests and the elders bribed the tomb guards to say, "His disciples came by night and stole him away while we were asleep." The eleven disciples went to Galilee and Jesus appeared to them and said, "All authority in heaven and on earth is given to me. Go therefore and make disciples of all nations baptizing them in the name of the Father and the Son and the Holy Spirit, teaching them to obey everything that I have commanded you. And remember, I am with you always, to the end of the age" (Matthew 28:18–20). In Luke 24:40–41, Jesus appeared, showed his wounds, asked for a piece of fish, and ate it. In John 21, Jesus appeared and helped the disciples achieve a large catch of fish, shared a shore breakfast with the disciples after they recognized him, and Jesus asked Peter three times to reaffirm his faith.

After these resurrection appearance stories, the followers of Jesus gradually regrouped, continuing to be influenced by the teachings of Jesus and the community of people who had responded to his teaching (Acts 2). At the annual Pentecost celebration, a group of them were gathered in an upper room in Jerusalem. Jesus was gone, but his spirit and teachings continued to influence his followers. While they were in that upper room, a religious experience took place that excited them so much that they went into the streets talking about it. Peter, one of the disciples of Jesus, preached a sermon interpreting the experience to the gathered people. Excitement grew, and a Hebrew church was formed in homes (Acts 8:1–4).

In Acts 9:1–31, a Hebrew Pharisee from Tarsus named Saul was on his way to Damascus to shut down this sector of the followers of the way of Jesus. He planned to arrest the leaders of the movement but on the road a lightning strike threw him to the ground, temporarily blinding him. In this state, he said he had an inner vision of Jesus asking him, "Saul, why do you persecute me?" A man named Ananias led him to Damascus and helped him recover, and he regained his sight. The experience changed or converted him. His name was changed from Saul to Paul, and he became a missionary of the movement establishing churches throughout the Middle East. In Jerusalem, at a conference with the disciple, Peter, who was accepted as the foremost authority for the new churches, Paul and Timothy, his helper, had a major break with tradition by including non-Jews in the groups that were forming. (Acts 11:1–18)

Letters from Paul and others, along with collections of the stories about Jesus and his preaching and teaching, were collected and preserved, valued, and passed around among these communities that came to be referred to as Christian. These grew even as they went through many difficulties and persecutions, and then, under the Emperor Constantine in the Third Century, Christianity became the official religion of the Roman Empire.

Whatever Jesus meant to people during his life did not die with him. A remarkable resurrection experience took place around this local martyred rabbi that evolved into a major world religion. The spirit of Jesus was still alive and available for inspiration and guidance for his followers. The fact that church has continued to this day attests to that.

Today we need to set aside the idea that the resurrection stories are about some other future life for believers. Instead it points to the possibility of new life in the faith possible to us in the here and now. I believe that is what the resurrection is really all about. The reality is that the power and influence of the risen Christ is still present now enabling us to discover and live more full and meaningful lives today. In other words, through the influence of Christ and his teachings we also can experience a change in our living so profound that it can only be described as a resurrection experience.

The very existence of the church today, with all its various interpretations of the myths and metaphors, is proof of Jesus's resurrection reality. This mythology focuses on the new life the faith can bring to us in the present. This is what the resurrection is really all about. The power of the risen Christ is that his influence is still present, enabling us to find more meaningful lives today.

WHAT IS ETERNAL LIFE?

One of the best-known and best-loved passages of scripture is "For God so loved the world that he gave his only Son so that everyone who believes in him may not perish but may have eternal life" (John 3:16). Eternal life is participation in God's life. God is eternal, and people share in eternity as they relate to the eternal one. For Christians, our relationship to God comes through our relationship to Jesus. This relationship to God through Jesus is experienced in the present life and relates us to all eternity. It is about being eternally alive, right now. It is not a next world, after death, exclusive, but a present world experience. It gives a new dimension of meaning to existence in all we do and are here and now. Jesus, in John 10:10, says, "I came that they may have life and have it abundantly." The impact of learning from Jesus produces in his disciples the experience of abundant living. Eternal life does not have to do with living forever. People are not eternal, but God is. We can understand Jesus's promise in John 3:16 and John 10 to mean eternal and abundant life is now, and links us up with the eternal God now.

What does Jesus mean when he says, "I am the way and the truth and the life? No one comes to the Father except by me." (John 14:6) These words of Jesus have been misused to claim Christianity as the only valid religion and assertions of belief in him as the only way to relate to God. A more meaningful way to understand and interpret these words of Jesus to Thomas and other disciples is, If you want to know the way into a relationship with God and to understand the true meaning of life, relate to God as I have related to God. Seek his guidance and live in relationship to him as a son or daughter to a good father. Follow my style and pattern of faithfulness as the way to go. Follow me and you will come to understand God's truth and patterns for life, I, Jesus, am the word of God made personal. I have opened and shown the way.

This statement is an invitation instead of an exclusion. It is not a condemnation of other faiths or religions, which seek God and his will for living in slightly different ways. Jesus lived as a representative Son of God by his obedience and acceptance of his relationship to God and enables us all to become children of God. It is Jesus's way of offering himself as a model. He acts as an intermediary, or channel, for God's mercy and acceptance of us. Jesus's submission to God's will in his life and ministry makes all acceptable to God. The love and mercy of God is for the world and none of us has earned it, but God grants it to us anyway. Our part is to respond to it and become part of the family of gratitude. The majority of the world's people may be like the nine lepers Jesus healed. All ten were healed, but only one came back to express gratitude and receive an additional blessing. The church is the grateful minority, the family of gratitude who, having been healed, act as healing agents in the reconciliation of the world.

WHY DO CHRISTIANS GATHER TOGETHER ON SUNDAY?

Sunday, the day after the Jewish Sabbath, was the day the followers of Jesus experienced the resurrection appearances, and so they came together to remember this on the first day of the week. They gathered in homes to worship God and share their experiences. Worship, by definition, means, primarily, to ascribe worth to God. The early Christians did this in accordance with the customary practices of the Hebrew synagogue with some modifications as they related to Jesus. These gatherings included singing and chanting words of adoration of God, and confessing of their personal weaknesses, and selfishness, called sin. They offered thanks for God's grace and acceptance of them, reading and seeking guidance from the writings of the faith community, through their experience of worship. They also ate meals together, breaking bread and drinking wine, the juice of local grapes. This later became a symbolic meal or time of communion referred to as the Last Supper, because Jesus asked his disciples for their remembrance of him in connection with this particular meal in his final days with them.

When new persons joined these gatherings, they were baptized with water, recalling the baptism of Jesus by John and symbolizing their spiritual birth and entrance into the faith community. This baptism replaced the Hebrew rite of circumcision and was a sign of entering into a covenant of discipleship to Jesus. Every new Christian became one who learned from Jesus's example of faithfulness with all promising to become learners or disciples. As time went on, parents made this promise on behalf of their young or infant children.

In addition to hearing and learning from the word preached and taught, those who gathered shared in a loyalty commitment patterned after the "sacramentum," which Roman soldiers took as a pledge of loyalty and commitment to the Roman army at the time of their enlistment. These meals together became a symbolic meal, the Lord's Supper, the Sacrament or promise of loyalty to Jesus as Lord of their lives. The worshippers prayed or communed with God as they experienced the fellowship of the meal, and were grateful for this experience and what happened in their lives. The four words of emphasis for the early gatherings in the emerging church were the Lord's Supper for the fellowship, Sacrament for the renewal of loyalty to Christ, Communion for prayer to God, and Eucharist, meaning giving thanks as an expression of gratitude to God.

Two sacraments emerged in the early church. Baptism, where discipleship to Christ was promised, and the Lord's Supper, where this promise was regularly renewed and confirmed. The sacraments are symbols or signs of the inner grace of

God at work in the lives of the participating worshippers, and modern worship, in all its forms, developed from those ancient practices.

WHAT IS THE PURPOSE OF WORSHIP?

There is a lot of misunderstanding about worship today that can benefit from clarification. In worship, as the word is preached and the sacraments administered, the involved participants are God, and worship leaders such as the pastor and liturgists, the organist and musicians, the choir, soloists, and praise teams, liturgical dancers, dramatists, church officers, teachers, and children. In the midst of this variety of participants, the modern worshiper is tempted to lapse into being the audience or spectator viewing a show, and to cease worshipping in favor of being entertained. In authentic worship, the congregation members are the actors, and the pastor, choirs, organist, soloists, liturgists, and all who appear in the pulpit, lectern, choir loft, or chancel are the prompters, or helping leaders. They are not actors or entertainers. They are there to facilitate the involvement of the participating worshipping congregation in their realization and recognition of God, who is the audience receiving the worship. Viewing worship as a show tends to demean it into theatrics or performance and turn it into a secular experience that is people-centered rather than God-centered. (2)

This is difficult to understand in today's world, since we are so used to being spectators. It makes this understanding more important than ever if we are not to become a godless or self-centered society. Applauding a sermon, choir anthem, or children's pageant focuses on the persons who are the leaders or prompters, placing them in center stage and pitting them against one another to see who is best. To God, all worship is acceptable and equal. It is not appropriate to single out any one part as better or more pleasing than any other. True worship keeps in mind that God is the audience and all the worshippers are the actors. Authentic adoration, confession, thanksgiving, and supplication in church affect our actions in life when we go out from worship to service in the world. This is why the ancient Christians came together on Sundays, and why we still gather together on the first day of the week. We are bringing the ancient story of Jesus's Sunday resurrection into the contemporary here and now and our relationship to the living Christ into today's experiences. This helps us find answers to life's urgent questions as we apply it in our lives.

HOW DO YOU EXPLAIN THE TRINITY AND WHAT DOES IT MEAN TO US?

The Trinity is about how God becomes known to us. We experience and think of God first as God, the one involved in the creation of the universe, and then as a set apart or Holy Spirit and third as Jesus. The Hebrew word for God is Elohim, but another word they used was Yahweh. Translated roughly, this means "the one who causes to be." This creator is linked to the spirit or wind of God, the "Ruah," in the very first verse of the Bible, "the wind from God swept over the waters" (Genesis 1). The word, "wind" was used because although you cannot see the wind, you see the actions and results of it in such things as swaying tree branches or waves in the water. God could not be seen, but the results of the spirit's actions could be seen and experienced. This is described in a word picture as the spirit sweeping over the face of the watery chaos to begin the formation of the earth. God is the creative force that causes all to be, but this becomes known and experienced through what is called the Spirit. Jesus is linked to God as his word or message to people made personal and tangible in the form of a human baby born to Mary. According to the Gospel of John, the word became flesh to dwell among us.

There is only one God in the Christian Biblical view, but God is made known by Word and Spirit. The creator God comes as word to us through the insightful writings of Priest and Prophet in the Old Covenant writings. When this word went unheeded or was unclear the incarnation or enfleshment of that word assumed human personality to enhance our understanding and reach us more effectively. In Jesus's life and teachings the words from the past come alive in a new way. He becomes the personification of those words. The writings of those who preached and taught in his name, because Jesus himself left no written record behind, continue to help us receive the message of God through the Spirit of all that Jesus was when he walked the earth.

We think of God as Father, Son, and Holy Spirit. God is recognized and experienced as (1) creative life source, (2) incarnate or embodied word that walked the earth like us, and (3) still living and influencing present moment counselor and guide. God is not a being among other beings, but is understood by us in the Trinitarian concept of revelation by God, through the written word, the incarnate word, and the Spirit word, which is all around each one of us in our lives to this day. Father, Son, and Holy Spirit are the various facets or faces of God's being. They are the ways we understand, sense, and experience the timeless God as a reality in our lives.

WAS JESUS A PERFECT HUMAN BEING?

If Jesus was the incarnation of God's word to us, then his life was special. The key question is, How was he special? Does this mean that he never made any human errors or had to struggle in his relationship to God? Was he God merely masquerading as a human being? Some of the descriptions in the Biblical New Covenant literature shed some light on this important question. In Luke 2:41–51, we have the story of Jesus as a boy going off inconsiderately without notifying his parents that he would be at the temple listening to and questioning the Jewish teachers. They had to stay behind and search for him. In Mathew 21:12, it is recorded that "he drove out all who were buying and selling in the temple, and he overturned the tables of the money changers and the seats of those who sold doves." These are violent, angry actions by any standard, and not the behavior of a meek, gentle man. In Mark 11:13, Jesus cursed a fig tree for not having any fruit when he was hungry, even though it was not the season for bearing fruit. This was an unfair and angry reaction, not really calling for a cursing of the tree. In the Garden of Gethsemane, Mark 14:32-42, he was depressed and angry with his closest disciples when they fell asleep while he agonized in prayer. In Mark 15:34, when he was suffering and dying on the cross, he was depressed. He felt and expressed bitterness and resentment toward God. Jesus said in Mark 10:18, "No one is good but God alone." Jesus was not perfect or free of human emotions and weaknesses, but through it all and in spite of everything he never broke relationship with God. Jesus identified himself with humanity and was not perfect. His relationship to God remained always intact. This was the mark of his goodness and perfection, which made him a model human being.

WHAT DOES IT MEAN TO BE HUMAN?

There are many species of creatures on earth, but humans are the only ones who can bind time, recording and cataloguing what they have learned. Humans, through cooperation, can develop culture and technology, preserving its complexities from generation to generation. Because it is written down and preserved in detail, it builds upon itself and accelerates exponentially with each generation. Other primates closely related to humans can learn from their parents and proceed through life according to their instincts and what they have learned. Chimpanzees use primitive tools such as stones and sticks. Primates can learn sign language, but cannot preserve their learning in a library. A polar bear cub learns survival patterns from its mother, and without this passing down from mother to cub the species would become extinct. Humans are not as dependent upon parent-to-offspring teaching and the trial and error relearning of each generation, as is the rest of the animal kingdom. Humanity understands the nature of the universe in ever-increasing depth. The work of human genius in such persons as Isaac Newton, Michael Faraday, Albert Einstein, or Charles Darwin make for an understanding of the universe beyond the comprehension of other planetary life forms. The heroes and mythology of various cultures enrich humanity and model what it means to be an authentic human being who has risen above self-centered survival living. Prophets and gifted leaders such as Moses, Muhammad, and Jesus illustrate the capabilities of human existence and provide patterns and examples of quality human lives. Relating to them and learning from them makes us authentically fully human, enabling us to rise to the level of what we each are created to be.

IS SEXUAL INTERCOURSE INTENDED ONLY FOR PROCREATION?

In the creation story in Genesis, the priestly writer points out that God said to humankind, "Be fruitful and multiply" (Genesis 1:28). This is a way of saying sex is a necessary way of continuing and multiplying the species and is there for the purpose of procreation. In the second creation myth, the writer has God say, "It is not good that the man should be alone. I will make him a helper as his partner." Sex then, is related to companionship and partnering, in addition to its necessity for the continuation of the species. Most of the higher mammals in the world engage in sex only when the female is in estrus, and for them sex is primarily for procreation. In humans, sex is voluntary and regulated by interest. It does not depend solely on the hormones but has a loving and recreational component in addition to the hormonal drive toward procreation. Human sexual intercourse is different from the sexuality of other species. It is related to love and companionship, two people becoming one and "knowing" each other.

Our society has become rather obsessed with this subject and lost sight of the fact that it is a gift from God enabling people to be closely interrelated with each other so they are not alone and lonely. In some people, the genes or brain makeup causes an attraction to their same sex. This is termed homosexuality, and is natural for these persons. They do not learn such attractions, but rather are born with them. They are inherent in their personality and desires. If sex relationships are natural between human males and females, it is also natural for these humans to experience same-sex attraction, which probably cannot be programmed out of their basic orientation by counseling or conversion. These drives, for them, are apparently as natural, and God-given, as heterosexual drives are natural and God-given for the majority of people. Homosexuality is not contagious or learned behavior, and as long as same-sex activity it is not abusive of children and is between mature consenting individuals it should not be unfairly judged as wrong or perverted and called a sin. The pleasures of sexual intercourse in humans are a gift from God, taking many forms. Sex was indeed for procreation to continue the species, but it is more than that. For the Christian it is for knowing your partner intimately as an expression of love for another and is a source of satisfying physical pleasure and enjoyment. It is also, most profoundly, a spiritual bonding under God, Christ, and the Holy Spirit "to be held in honor by all" as stated in the church wedding vows.

WHY DO THE WICKED PROSPER AND THE INNOCENT SUFFER?

The wicked don't always prosper, but when we see this happening it offends our innate sense of justice, and we blame God. We expect to be rewarded by God for our good behavior and bad behavior punished. God should know enough to do it right. Jesus's words were, "You have heard that it was said, 'You shall love your neighbor and hate your enemy' but I say to you, Love your enemies and pray for those who persecute you, so that you may be children of your father in heaven; for he makes his sun rise on the evil and on the good, and sends rain on the righteous and the unrighteous." (Mathew 5:43-44) This is a way of saying that God's goodness is for all and the order of the universe requires uniform treatment in accord with natural law. The laws of nature prevail in the world for the general good of all, but many become victims of these same laws. We wish it were not so, but exceptions are not made when weather patterns bring hurricanes and tornadoes or when illness or infection takes human life. Evil persons can gain the upper hand through chance or exploitation and, though good actions do have payoff in the long run, there are many exceptions along the way. Free will can lead to wrong decisions, which often have unwanted consequences, and the innocent may suffer, not only from their own actions but also because of the actions of others beyond their control. The paradigm of Christianity is that Jesus did not escape suffering and an unjust execution, but his resurrected presence in the lives of his followers brought into being a new religious hero and a saving presence in the world. Our faith can help us find goodness and meaning even in the worst of circumstances. God's spirit works for good, and the power of faith enables us to cope with even the worst of the evils of the world.

IS THE WORLD ABOUT TO END, AND WILL JESUS COME AGAIN?

A part of the mythology of the early church was that Jesus would soon return to earth in the clouds. "Then they will see 'the Son of Man coming in the clouds with great power and glory. Then he will send out the angels, and gather his elect from the four winds, from the ends of the earth to the ends of heaven." (Mark 13:26–27) This reference to a second coming of Jesus occurs in other places in scripture, most notably in the last book of the New Covenant, the book of Revelation. One of the problems with our understanding of these Biblical texts is that we have frequently linked them with the predicting of future events. The original purpose of Revelation was to immediately encourage the community of Christians who were suffering under the pressure of persecution from the Roman Emperor, Domition. Because parts of the writings in the book referred to the Emperor in a negative way, many symbolic and code words were used which would not be understood outside the Christian community. This protected any who would be caught with the writings from being put to death for sedition against Rome. The Emperor, for instance, was referred to as a beast and not named. The message to those who were being singled out for persecution was one of hope and encouragement. God was described as the alpha and omega, or beginning and end, who was ultimately in control of the earth. The references were not designed to point to the distant future in a specific way but, rather, addressed present circumstances in the Christian community of the day in a cryptic way.

Over the years this obscure Biblical imagery has been used as a prediction of a doomsday scenario. In 1832, after ten years of Bible study and meditation, and conversing with his neighbors, a farmer and minister, William Miller, publicly spoke convincingly about the glorious Second Coming of the Lord Jesus Christ and predicted that this would happen between 1843 and 1844. The followers of Miller published the date, but when the great day arrived nothing happened. This was a great blow to his followers. They have become the Adventist sects. This doomsday talk and accompanying manner of Biblical interpretation should have died with the discouraged and disillusioned Miller and those who preceded him, but it lingers on. In recent times, the preaching of William Miller morphed into fundamentalist Hal Lindsey's book "The Late Great Planet Earth," a best-seller filled with erroneous Biblical interpretations. In it, he predicted that a coming war in the Middle East over oil would be the first step in the ending of the world and lead to the Second Coming of Christ. The anti-Christ was the Soviets or the leaders of the U.N. Now the Muslims have been put in this role, as we are involved in another war in the Middle East, partially over oil, and the end has not yet come. The doomsday predictions have come to naught, but the influence of this thinking is still very pervasive, making it difficult for people to discern what the Biblical message really has to offer.

The earth still orbits around the sun, and day follows day. We could pollute the planet until it could no longer support life. We could unleash nuclear forces, and bring on nuclear winter. Probably the world is going to end someday, perhaps billions of years from now when the sun no longer produces enough energy to sustain life on our planet, or swells into a giant star and burns the surface of our planet. But this has little or no connection to Biblical understanding, except in the sense that Christians need to be responsible for helping maintain the life of God's good earth and the people who live on it whenever and wherever possible.

Millerite thinking and the book of Revelation surfaced again quite recently, causing a big stir in and through a series of twelve popular end-time novels about the rapture culture by Jerry Jenkins and a Baptist minister, Tim Lahaye. They describe, in fictional form, the secret return of Jesus to transport all believers into heaven, with cars, trains, and planes flying into each other as believers are suddenly taken to heaven, leaving their clothes, cars, and even their dental fillings behind. A bumper sticker began to appear in local traffic: "Warning. In case of rapture this vehicle will be unmanned." This view, termed dispensationalism, holds to the idea that after seven years of dealing with anti-Christ and international wars there is to be a final violent battle against evil on the plain of Armageddon in Israel, and then Jesus will come on a cloud and straighten it all out.

Early Christians were understandably discouraged that Jesus didn't return on a cloud in their time, as they believed he would, and their mythology broke down on this issue. They did not recognize that the Biblical description of Jesus's second coming was already realized when his spirit entered their lives and hearts. The perception of the meaning of Jesus and his life leading to awareness and learning that led to a relationship with him and his teachings was a second coming. Jesus comes again every time the awareness of him and his meaning becomes perceived by someone, and Jesus doesn't have to come on a cloud for there to be an effective second coming in believers' hearts, one person at a time. It has already happened, and continues to happen over and over again. Jesus returns when his spirit enters our lives. God is not a terrorist who surprises us with bloody interventions into history and Jesus, our hero and savior, was not a warrior. He made his triumphal entry into Jerusalem on a donkey, a beast of burden, not a warhorse, and God is not an unforgiving judge, waiting to convict us of wrongdoing. In Jesus of Nazareth we live under the grace of God made personal. His mythological life and death bring us into an understanding of being at one with God, who graciously forgives our selfishness though our faith and discipleship as we learn from the example of Jesus as he returns again into our lives. God in and through Christ is with us from alpha to omega, from A to Z, or from the beginning to the end. Jesus has already come and accomplished all that is necessary for our salvation and for the fullness of living available to us in the years of our life. He continues to come daily into our lives again and again, and into the lives of others until the end of time. We need to cherish each day that we live as a gift from God. The world will not end soon, but for each of us our time will run out, Our life in the world as we know it does come to an end, but this is not the second coming of Jesus. The coming of Jesus takes place in our lives whenever we experience him in our life. When we become aware of this Jesus becomes real again and the second coming has already occured for us even if we fail to notice or recognize it.

HOW CAN RELIGION HELP US IN THE WORLD TODAY?

Religion can profoundly change our lives, and through us others can also be helped. There are varieties of religious experiences based on different faith heroes and mythologies. All are helpful, but some are more so than others. I believe in the Christian faith, and it has proven itself to me through the years; I have attempted to answer the preceding questions from a Christian evaluative worldview. These questions are some which come to mind as I attempt to translate sacred myths and metaphors in a post mythological and metaphorical time. Most myths, including Christian myths, are not literal, factual truth, but neither are they lies. They convey deep, profound truths, which are applicable in our lives and affect and direct our worldview. If you attempt to make a myth into a literal fact, you make it irrelevant and unbelievable. If you take a religious story, myth, or metaphor as a way of conveying meaning and understanding of a point about the nature of a life of faith, it can be of profound help in understanding not only the point made but also a larger meaning and purpose to life itself. It can lead us to discover how God can direct and change our lives for the better. For the Christian who wants to keep on believing in an unbelieving and secular world, we are enabled to continue and deepen our belief as we understand the nature of our sacred writings, and their stories, myths, and reflections on religious experience without casting our mind and reason aside. We only need to grasp what we truly have in our faith heroes and stories and mythologies in the sacred literature. Paul, the apostle, said in II Corinthians 5:17, "So if anyone is in Christ, there is a new creation: everything old has passed away; everything has become new." He said that being influenced by Christ in our lives changes everything right down to the core of our being. Christ is our faith hero and we are his disciples, those who learn from him. He keeps us on track in life and leads us to feel acceptance by God. He says in II Corinthians 5:18–19, "God in Christ has reconciled the world," and calls us to discover joy in our reconciliation and acceptance and, under God's grace, to participate in the reconciliation of others.

WHY THE CHURCH?

The Greek word for church is "eklesia," which means "that which is called out." So the church is made up of those who are called out from the people of the world to be a community of disciples of Jesus the anointed one. As we respond to this calling to be people learning from Jesus, we are led to minister to others in the name of Jesus. In the church fellowship we come to know what it means to experience the abundant life and joy of relationship to Jesus and his modern disciples. As we learn from Jesus and the Holy Spirit's influence, we move beyond being just students of the faith to serving God by becoming ministers or apostles in the church and the world. So wherever we are and whatever we are doing, Jesus and God's Holy Spirit are present through us. So we move from becoming disciples of Jesus and members of his Spirit-directed church to being modern-day apostles. Richard Avery and Donald Marsh said it well in the song. "The church is not a building. The church is not a steeple. The church is not a resting place. The church is the People. I am the church. You are the church. We are the church together. All who follow Jesus, all around the world. Yes we're the church together." (3) The church is all of us, past, present, and future. We are all ministers. We are the contemporary arms, legs, hands, feet, and voices of Jesus in the modern world. We, the people together, are the church.

HOW CAN WE FIND GOD'S WILL FOR OUR LIVES?

God's will has two parts: a general will for all people and the world, and a particular calling and niche for everyone related to him. Our life joy is to discover what we love doing in the world, our particular calling. The guidance of Christ and the church can help us discover our calling and respond to God in fulfilling this calling. Everyone has a calling and can discover God's specific will for their living of life. Discovering this is how religion can help us in our life today. While we were visiting our grandson at Florida Atlantic University, he wanted to show us a potential rental for his next year of college. But all he had was the address. He entered the address in a Magellan GPS and plugged it into the car outlet. We left the university parking lot and the GPS's female voice gave me complete directions: where and when to turn, even calling for a U turn if it was legal, when I missed a turn, and telling me when we had arrived at the house. In a similar fashion, God has a guidance system for our lives, giving directions through the example of Jesus, his church, and the Holy Spirit. When we plug our interests and skills into God's guidance system like we plug into the GPS, we will be directed to God's will for us. If we follow our joys to discover our niche and respond to God's call day by day, we will be amazed at what the Lord will do through us.

There was a man named Fleming who was a poor Scottish farmer, probably a Presbyterian Christian. One day, while trying to make a living for his family, he heard a cry for help coming from a nearby bog, so he dropped his tools and ran to it. There, mired to his waist in black muck, was a terrified boy screaming and struggling to free himself. Farmer Fleming saved the lad from what could have been a slow and terrifying death. The next day, a carriage pulled up to the Scotsman's sparse surroundings, and an elegantly dressed nobleman stepped out and introduced himself as the father of the boy Fleming had saved. "You saved my son's life and I want to repay you," said the nobleman, but the Scottish farmer waved him off, saying, "No, I canna accept payment for what I did." At that moment, the farmer's own son came to the door of the family hovel, and the nobleman asked, "Is that your son?" The farmer proudly replied, "Yes," and the nobleman said,

"I'll make you a deal. Let me provide him with the level of education my own son will enjoy, and if the lad is anything like his father he'll no doubt grow into a man we can both be proud of." Farmer Fleming's son attended the very best schools of his time, and graduated from St. Mary's Hospital school in London. He went on to become known throughout the world as the noted Sir Arthur Fleming, the discoverer of penicillin. Years afterward, the same nobleman's son saved from the bog was stricken with pneumonia, and this time it was penicillin which saved his life. The name of the nobleman was Lord Randolph Churchill and the name of his son Sir Winston Churchill.

World history would have been different if youthful Winston had sunk into the bog and died, or later died of pneumonia in the hospital without the penicillin discovered by the farmer's son. We never know what the effect of a faith-based act may be or how far reaching it may be in the hands of God. This is an example of what Presbyterians call predestination: not that our destinies are predetermined with no freedom of choice, but, rather, that we can look back and discern the hand of God in our lives.

Faith translated into caring actions, bit by bit can save the world or make it a better place. Biblical beliefs understood and acted upon can and do help us in the world today. If we seek God's will for our lives it will be made known to us. As an old-fashioned church solo puts it, "It is no secret what God can do. What he's done for others he'll do for you." Albert Schweitzer, an acclaimed university music professor and organist, and a renowned theologian, gave it all up to study medicine and become a missionary doctor in Africa. Albert Schweitzer explained his decision this way: "To know the will of God is the greatest knowledge, to accept the will of God is the greatest heroism, to do the will of God is the greatest achievement, to have the approval of God on your work is the greatest happiness."

CONCLUDING REMARKS

What I have written is not intended to be definitive or final, but if it has helped answer some questions about the faith, which have occurred to you in your faith journey, or has given you a different perspective on some of the issues raised, it will have been a successful endeavor on my part. It is my hope that it will stimulate you to raise and reflect on further questions. The journey to faith is a lifelong quest, a search for your personal destiny in your own world and time, and the rewards can be immensely gratifying. In the words of Paul from Ephesians 3:20 and 21, "Now to him who by the power at work within us is able to accomplish abundantly far more than all we can ask or imagine, to him be glory in the church and in Christ Jesus to all generations, forever and ever. Amen."

NOTES

All scriptures referred to or quoted are from The New Oxford Annotated Bible, New Revised Standard Version, 1991, New York, Oxford University Press.

(1) "The Future of an Illusion," Sigmund Freud, Liveright Publishing Company, 1923, New York, pp. 41–42.

(2) "Purity of Heart Is to Will One Thing," Sören Kierkegaard, Harper Torchbooks, Harper & Brothers Publishers, 1956, New York, pp. 177–181.

(3) "We Are the Church," copyright 1972, Hope Publishing Company, Carol Stream, Ill.

Cover design: "Jonah in the Whale," by Nicholas of Verdun. Detail of the Verduner altarpiece in Klosterneuburg, Austria.

ABOUT THE AUTHOR

Dr. Dale Heaton is a PCUSA pastor who retired in 1994, after forty years in parish ministry. He experienced his call to the ministry under the leadership of Dr. Harrison Ray Anderson of Fourth Presbyterian Church in Chicago, Illinois, and was ordained in 1954, while serving First Presbyterian Church of Des Plaines, Illinois, a new development congregation he organized after graduation from Northwestern University (Ph.B) and McCormick Seminary (M.Div.) under the auspices of Chicago Presbytery. The next five years he was part of Southern Michigan Presbytery leading a church in Edwardsburg, Michigan. During this time he received continuing education by attending three new pastors' training seminars sponsored by the denomination and a preaching seminar led by Dr. George Buttrick, as well as graduate stuudy at Western Michigan University. His next pastorate was Ottawa, Illinois (Blackhawk Presbytery), where he served nine years and began his study at San Anselmo Seminary in San Francisco, leading to a Doctor of Ministry degree in 1978.

A twenty-two year ministry with Presbyterian Church of Titusville, Florida, began in 1971, where he also served as Stated Clerk for Northeast Florida and then Central Florida Presbytery, where he was part of the committee for merger of the two denominations in 1983. In 1984, as President of the Florida Council of Churches, he participated in a peacemaking mission, which met and visited with churches, city government officials, and peacemaking groups in major cities throughout the Soviet Union. In 1986 he took part in a two-week Middle

East Study group, traveling Jordan and Israel meeting with and talking to Palestinian and Israeli leaders. In 1989, he traveled to Japan for several weeks with his son, who was fluent in the language and culture of that part of the world. In 1990, he participated in a three-month-long Scotland pulpit exchange, where he served three historic little churches in Creich, Kilmaney, and Monimail in County Fife, and traveled throughout the country under the guidance of a well versed native Scotsman.

In the course of his ministry, he attended five general assemblies, serving as delegate for two. Since retirement in 1994, he has served three interim pastorates and continues to be active in Central Florida Presbytery in various capacities. He is Pastor Emeritus in the First Presbyterian Church of Titusville, where he and his wife, Jane, reside, and are active in church and community. They raised a family of six children and have seven grandchildren living in Florida, North Carolina, and New York City.

December 2010

www.ingramcontent.com/pod-product-compliance
Ingram Content Group UK Ltd.
Pitfield, Milton Keynes, MK11 3LW, UK
UKHW020236250726
13967UKWH00001B/399

9 781435 793965